Baghdad Blues

DAVID TURNLEY

Baghdad Blues

A WAR DIARY

A MARK MAGOWAN BOOK
VENDOME · NEW YORK

INTRODUCTION

On the last day of the first Gulf War in 1991, I made a photograph of a young soldier being evacuated in a helicopter, grieving as he realized that the man in a body bag next to him was his best friend. The soldiers in this photograph had been in a Bradley fighting vehicle that was hit by friendly fire close to An Nasiriya near the Euphrates River. I had spent months positioning myself to photograph the work of the elite MASH unit that was evacuating this young soldier, and I deeply respected the work of these trauma doctors and nurses. I also knew that documenting their work would put me in acute proximity to the war, and, in the case of this unit, without a public affairs officer to control what I could photograph. The Pentagon pool restrictions in 1991 had been explicit in attempting to prevent photojournalists from making the kind of images that had effectively helped to turn public opinion against the war in Vietnam by so poignantly revealing the human cost of military conflict. I have always believed that no matter what one's political position, we all need to be clear about the human cost of war.

I had made a personal decision three years ago that I would not cover war again. That changed on September 11, 2001, when I walked out of my apartment on Tenth Street in Greenwich Village and the first of two planes hit the World Trade Center. It took me only a few seconds to realize that I had no choice but to grab my cameras and head down to the war zone that was in my backyard to continue doing the work that I know how to do.

In Iraq in 1991, U.S. Sergeant Ken Kozakiewicz cries as he learns that the body bag next to him in the medical evacuation helicopter contains his friend killed by friendly fire.

It was because of my experiences dealing with the Pentagon restrictions during the first Gulf War and other recent conflicts—in Grenada and Panama, for example—that I was determined not to be an "embedded" photojournalist in this war. I say that as I acknowledge that many of my embedded colleagues, whom I greatly respect, made some of the most dramatic and poignant photographs in the history of war.

On September 11, 2002, a New York fireman stares ahead atop the rubble only hours after two planes brought down the World Trade Center.

In February I was given an extraordinary opportunity by Eason Jordan of CNN to go the gulf region, where I served as a correspondent mixing video, photography, and on-air reporting. My brief early on was to work in the surrounding countries and along the border of Iraq to tell stories of people who were in some way affected by Saddam Hussein's regime, and to put a human face on the population of the region.

For the first month and a half of my three months in the Middle East for CNN, I worked in Syria and then in Turkey in the Kurdish-controlled area along the border of Iraq. As the war approached, our plan was to be in a position to enter northern Iraq, which was held by the Kurds, and to eventually get to Baghdad to cover the war from there. The only two ways to get into northern Iraq were through Iran or through Turkey, but both routes were shut off—officially, at least. I couldn't get a visa from Iran, and the Turks would not allow me to cross their border legally. For the first time in my twenty years of covering conflict, I resorted to being smuggled, first into Syria and from there into northern Iraq. This is where my story begins.

When I returned to the Middle East this year on the eve of another war, I decided that it was time for me to write a journal at the end of every day—it would be an opportunity to think carefully and fully about the work I do as a photojournalist. Perhaps I also felt that someday my son might want to know what his father experienced and felt while working. I quickly found that writing became my companion while living far from family and friends, sometimes lonely and often scared. I've always yearned for a world that transcends the divisions of gender, ethnicity, and nationality, and the diary I wrote helped me to think about what this means to my work as a photographer.

The photographs in this book were transmitted to CNN in Atlanta every day of the war, and many were seen on television, with me as narrator. *Baghdad Blues* is the culmination of my personal experience during this time. As a photographer, I am accustomed to communicating about the world visually, but in this book my words and images work together to convey the immensely human story of life during the war in Iraq.

3/20/03

I've spent three weeks making a plan to be smuggled from Turkey into northern Iraq. The initial attempt failed. Anticipating the first cruise missile attacks on Baghdad, thousands of refugees are on the run. I'm trying to go against the tide, arranging with smugglers to get me through Syria into the war zone, along with Pete, Mitch, and Chas, three ex-soldiers from British special forces who will be working as war zone consultants with CNN crews in northern Iraq.

The four of us are dropped off by car on the Turkish side near the banks of the Tigris River. Waiting for us are two peshmergas—Kurdish fighters—whom we met two nights before on our first stab at crossing the border. Paco, the lead peshmerga, is only about five feet four inches tall but one of the toughest men I've ever met. He is handsome in spite of his crooked front tooth, and he wears white Wellington rubber boots. We refer to him affectionately as "the Rat," because of his way of moving in a sharp, frenetic, purposeful way. He can lug a sixty-kilo equipment case on his shoulders with ease as he races through the mountains in the rain. Every ten minutes the ringer on his cell phone goes off to the tinny tune of "White Christmas."

Under a raging downpour, Paco and his companion Hamed lead us three and a half kilometers through fields, ravines, and hills, toward the Tigris River. We are constantly

Here I am photographing in a Kurdish shish-kebab restaurant in a small Turkish town on the way to the border with Iraq. PHOTOGRAPH BY JACK VAN ANTWERP

reminded to keep quiet and to not light cigarettes or illuminate our cell phones (although Paco's phone remains in a tuneful mode).

As we reach the river, we hide in the brush to avoid being spotted by Turkish soldiers in watchtowers. After about an hour, our smuggler, Hassan, and two other Kurd fighters from Syria pull up to the shore in an inflatable dinghy. I notice that their paddles are broken and the dinghy seems to have just enough space for two small children.

Hassan and his friend bark orders to the ex–special forces soldiers and me. We're to get on our knees in the dinghy, and the seven bags we're lugging are to be thrown on top of us. The peshmerga guides go up front to paddle the dinghy to the Syrian side of the river. We gingerly climb into the flimsy vessel, but Chas isn't happy with the arrangements and jumps out. We decide that Peter and I will cross first, and then our men will go back for Chas and Mitch.

Kurdish women dance during a wedding ceremony outside the Turkish village of Czire.

By now it's the middle of the night. I crouch in the dinghy along with Pete Hornett, a tall, physically fit man with the chiseled looks of a highly trained soldier, who will travel with me through northern Iraq in the coming days. Hassan and another peshmerga at the so-called helm steer us across the swollen Tigris; the current is flowing at more than eight knots, and they strain to keep the dinghy on its path toward the other side. Any minute now, I know, we'll capsize, and into the river I'll go, along with the $10,000 cash in my pocket, my passport, and all of my cameras and video equipment.

Rushing with the current downriver, we hit a patch of white-water rapids, and half the river seems to pour into the dinghy. Just when I think we're going under, we pass through the rapids and reach the Syrian side. Pete and I take shelter in a ravine while Hassan and company go back across the river for Chas and Mitch.

Eventually we're reunited: seven people and seven bags. Now we make our way by foot for six hundred meters on a track of compacted earth and rock. Then, in order to skirt a police outpost, we head into cultivated fields, through clay turned to muck by the torrential rain. For the next three hours, we slog through this mess, over wet rolling fields, to our pick-up point: a stack of brush piled on the side of the road. A one-and-a-half-ton light flatbed truck pulls up. With the help of my colleagues, I just manage to jump on board before it's on its jolting way, careering through the downpour along rutted country roads.

Sometime in the early morning, we arrive at a village and are hurried into a safe house—in fact, the home of Hassan, our Syrian smuggler. In a twenty-by-twelve-foot room covered with carpets, we are asked to remove our soiled and drenched clothes and mud-covered boots. We get a fleeting glimpse of Hassan's wife as she whisks everything off to be cleaned. With wet rags, we try to clean the mud from our gear bags.

Luckily, we get a call on our Thuraya, a fancy mobile satellite phone that can get through to any place from anywhere. It's our Kurdish fixer-translator Ibrahim back in Turkey. We also get calls through to our agencies in Atlanta and England. We tell them that after nightfall, we plan to cross yet another river, this time into Iraq.

Our peshmerga guides remove their kaffiyehs to reveal their faces as we sit companionably, sharing cigarettes. After we pay them their fee of $1,500 apiece, I trot out my rudimentary Arabic and laugh while introducing myself. The three men range in age from their thirties to forties. Two have ten children each.

Tea and food appear: warm, fresh pita with hummus, a sort of molasses soup, and yogurt with cucumber; it's one of the best and most appreciated meals I've had in days. Afterward, four mattresses are laid out on the floor, with blankets. Our Kurdish guides say goodbye. The rest of us, all seasoned, well-trained men, absolutely exhausted, quickly fall asleep.

I wake at 5:30 A.M. to the rattling snores of one of the Brits, whose mates are figuring out how to silence him. It's no use, and nobody can get back to sleep. At 6:00 I call CNN headquarters in Atlanta to discover that the war started thirty minutes ago. An American cruise missile hit a presidential palace, and anti-aircraft artillery is reportedly going off around Baghdad. There is other news: an attack on the northern Iraqi town of Mosul; chaos and panic among people trying to flee to Kuwait; a stream of refugees heading toward the Iraqi border.

We plan to hide in the safe house until nightfall, when we are to continue our trek and cross the Tigris into Iraq. On the other side, I hope to find waiting nine bags and cases of equipment that were supposed to have been

Kurdish children stand in the doorway of a home in the Turkish village of Handek, along the border with northern Iraq.

smuggled across two nights ago. I also hope to find a Kurdish driver and a four-wheel-drive vehicle (sent by a CNN producer in northern Baghdad) to take Pete and me south to cover the evolving war.

Mitch, a big, handsome New Zealander straight out of a James Bond film, quietly uses his Thuraya to call his eleven-year-old daughter. Last night before our crossing, I called Charlie, my nine-year-old son, in Capetown, South Africa. I wanted to tell him I love him.

Now, the night before setting off for northern Iraq, I cry, missing my beautiful son. I look forward to sitting with him and sharing the stories of this adventure, although I have always avoided details that could make him worry about me. There will be time for fear. So I talk about what I do as an adventure.

Our peshmerga friends interrupt my thoughts about Charlie. They have come to smoke more cigarettes and drink more tea. "America, England, Iraq—boom, boom," they tell us. We watch Syrian television showing scenes from the first morning of war. As the day wears on, I call the international desk at CNN every hour and ask them to put me on hold so I can listen to CNN radio for an update. Former defense secretary William Cohen is saying that three thousand cruise missiles will be unleashed on Baghdad, now, at the beginning of the war.

A Kurdish child stands in her family's home in Handek.

3/22/03

I am still in a safe house in Syria—a new one. It's been only forty-eight hours, but it seems like an eternity that I have been trying to get into northern Iraq. In my decades of covering war zones I've never experienced anything like the treacherous complexity of these travel arrangements.

Two nights ago, my three CNN colleagues and I left the house of the Syrian smuggler Hassan crammed in the back of a truck with all our gear. At the end of the bumpy ride, we were dumped in a freshly tilled, muddy cornfield. Our journey to the Tigris River began.

The mission had a bad feel from the start as rain cascaded from a dark evening sky and the air was frigid. About five minutes into what became a three-hour hike to the river in ankle-deep mud, Hassan lost the magazine to his AK-47. We waited for a half hour until he found it. The weight of our packs and our sodden feet and pants made the time seem longer.

Kurdish schoolchildren play outside their one-room schoolhouse in Handek.

When we finally made it to the river, we were met by two new peshmergas, who were supposed to take us in two dinghies two kilometers downriver into Kurdistan (the Kurd-controlled area of northern Iraq). But there was only one dinghy, and water flowing into the river from the nearby mountains after days of heavy rain made the river too high and dangerous for safe passage. We spent a couple of hours making phone calls back and forth to our Kurdish translator in Turkey, sorting out this new set of problems.

There also seemed to be an inter-Kurdish squabble slowing us down. It turned out that Hassan the Syrian belongs to a Kurdish faction opposed to the peshmerga guerrillas. We were able to surmise through our rudimentary Kurdish and Arabic that Hassan's parents had been killed because of their political affiliation. In revenge, Hassan had killed many peshmergas. Apparently, he will be killed if he enters Kurdistan. So he smuggles people out of Turkey and downriver to Kurdistan, but he will go no further.

Nobody felt comfortable when we saw the river, and the risk of capsizing and hypothermia was uppermost in our minds. So we trekked for two hours to another safe house in another village and we've been stuck here ever since.

Last night it was decided that Mitch, the New Zealander, and Chas, the Englishman—both strapping and tough as nails—would cross first and hook up with two other CNN crews inside Iraq. They left as planned and haven't come back, so we assume they made it. Pete and I are to follow tonight. With Hassan and the two peshmergas, we hike once again to the river—only to find more hours of inexplicable delay in the freezing cold rain. We return to the safe house.

At about 1:30 A.M., Pete is woken up by a phone call from Mitch, and so he wakes me. "There has been some drama," military parlance for "something life threatening." We learn that Mitch and Chas made it to Kurdistan after a seven-kilometer trek followed by a white-water raft trip down the river, then a portage through knee-deep swamp before a quick crossing into Kurdistan past Syrian-armed watchtowers. At the end, they were dumped in Kurdistan and forced to hide underneath a police station, where they're calling from, soaked and cold and not sure which is worse: to expose themselves to armed Kurdish police or to the elements and hypothermia.

There's a flurry of phone calls back and forth between them, us, our Kurdish fixer-translator Ibrahim, and "Blue Man"—another ex–special forces guy in Turkey—until everything gets sorted out. After they're assured the Kurdish police will be friendly, Mitch and Chas go into the station, only to have their passports confiscated. More phone calls. Our Kurdish safe house patron talks to the police, and by 5 A.M. our colleagues are in a motel in a small northern Iraqi town nearby.

A Kurdish woman packs down the mud roof of her family's home in Handek.

The previous night, Baghdad was heavily hit. American troops now occupy northern oil fields; the Turks, who we think have entered from the north, are making a mess in Kurdistan; and two English helicopters have collided in the Persian Gulf. My thoughts are interrupted by a phone call from my twin brother Peter's mother-in-law in Huron, Ohio. Peter, a photojournalist, is also in the region and she is concerned about both of us.

I would be lying if I said I too wasn't anxious about our trip tonight. Water and cold pose a different kind of threat than the war zone I'm about to enter—and curiously, water and cold seem less under my control. Meanwhile, I'm worrying about my equipment on the other side of the river; Hassan knows where it is but he won't give us an address for fear that the peshmergas will discover his safe house over there. He promises to send a coded message by phone, explaining everything to our local contact.

I keep in mind Pete's warning about the dangers of hypothermia as we prepare for the trip. I put on a thin pair of socks and a pair of running pants with two plastic bags over each leg and another pair of socks and pants to try to keep my feet dry. I'm ready to leave this room where I've spent the last four days staring at the ceiling fan overhead, at the cushions with Persian patterns lining the four bare walls, at the plastic flower arrangements in vases, and the life-size hand-drawn poster of the host family's daughter. We couldn't show our Western faces outside for fear of being discovered and arrested. We had to knock on the door when we wanted to use the toilet that I improvised—a bucket in a chicken coop.

Through Ibrahim in Turkey, we make final calls to our smuggler Hassan to find out if and where our equipment has been delivered inside Kurdistan. Hassan finally gives us the number of a man in a village, then asks for more money for our stay in the safe houses and for the peshmergas who will take us two kilometers down the river and across the swamp into Kurdistan.

For the third time, we head for the river. The trek through the darkness and the heavy mud feels all too familiar. This time, though, we carry less weight, and I've learned how to keep my feet dry.

A Kurdish family in Handek inside the tent that serves as their home.

On a slope overlooking the river, I put my left foot down into what turns out to be the edge of a fifty-foot ravine. Pete reaches down and grabs my hand, helping stop my slide. I am able to crawl and pull myself up over the steep muddy incline, and we move on.

By this time, the rain has stopped. We reach a point where the Tigris is very wide and fast, but calm enough for travel. We inflate the dinghy and set it in the river. One by one, the four of us get in and crouch at the bottom. I hunker down in the back. In front, the peshmergas push off with makeshift wooden paddles and we head downriver. One of them hands Pete a grenade and his Kalashnikov for safekeeping. After about forty-five minutes, we are forced to step waist-deep into the water and carry the dinghy across a five-hundred-meter swamp. We then get back in the boat and head out onto the water. Here, where two tributaries come together to make up the greater Tigris River, is the juncture of three countries—Turkey, Syria, and Iraq.

I finally find a way to sit on the back edge of the vessel so that my feet aren't getting numb. In this relatively comfortable position, I reflect that dangerous as the whole venture seems, at this moment, floating under the midnight stars in the middle of a quiet, fast-flowing river, knowing that my cameras are intact and that my

A Kurdish woman brings water from the well.

traveling companions are as tough as they come, I feel a profound sense of peace that I haven't experienced for ages.

But it doesn't last. We hit the beach, and the peshmergas whisper excitedly: "Kurdistan, Kurdistan." The owner of the Kalashnikov and the grenade reclaims them and points toward the Kurdish police station where, presumably, our two companions are waiting. Then he kisses me on both cheeks and shakes my hand.

I wake up in a small hotel in northern Iraq, lying in bed, remembering the previous night's reunion with my traveling mates, and still worrying about our nine bags of equipment. We had toasted our successful journey (and the end of at least this one ordeal) with Barbados rum and Coke, watching the BBC news reports, noting with dismay the many television reporters who seem to enjoy playing war. It reminds me of how disillusioned my point man was with some of the journalists embedded with the military units. Some have been sucked in hook, line, and sinker and are essentially serving as public relations reps for the United States Army. Even one of CNN's most seasoned correspondents announced from the field how much fun he was having with his army unit. And we're deeply disturbed and saddened by reports that four journalists may have been killed yesterday. That makes me also think about last night's conversation with my mother, who hasn't heard from my brother, Peter, who is on assignment for the *Denver Post* somewhere in southern Iraq.

3/24/03

I wake up this morning under pressure—to get south to Sulaimaniya. Our equipment has not yet been located. I've been told by CNN to cut my losses if I can't find it and travel the six hundred kilometers to the eastern border with Iran, to the place where an Australian journalist was killed by a car bomb. It's a Kurdish area adjacent to the camp of an Iranian fundamentalist Al Qaeda group. The idea is for me to do photographic reports for the Aaron Brown show and standup reporting for CNN.

We spend the morning at the local Kurdish police station. Suspecting that the police know where our equipment is, I offer a reward, and they tell me not to leave town until they get back to us. Not long afterward, I get a call that camera gear and satellite phones have shown up at a local governor's office in Dahuk. Interesting coincidence. Still, I'm ecstatic at the possibility of getting the gear back, and now things finally feel like they're coming together.

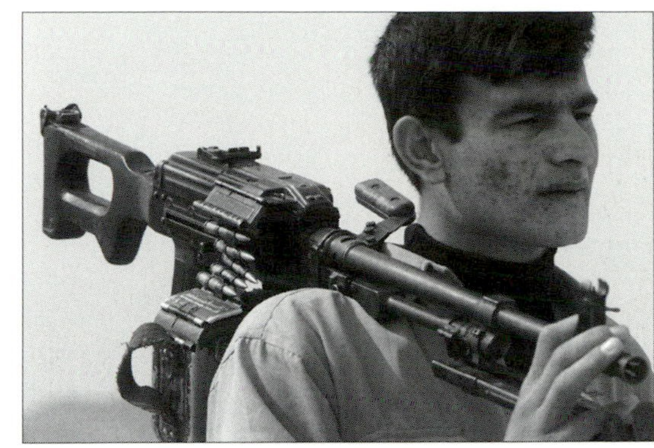

On the front line between pro-Saddam Iraqi forces and Kurdish fighters supported by American special forces, a Kurdish fighter stands near a bunker near Kifri in northern Iraq.

So the excursion of being smuggled across rivers from Turkey to Syria to Iraq has come to an end. Finally, we are summoned to the Dahuk governor's office in northern Iraq. When we arrive, the governor and his entourage greet us at the door. He is a small, solemn man with a wrinkled forehead that testifies to a life of responsibility and worry.

We are led down a corridor to his big office and politely asked to sit down. The governor soberly announces that his people have recovered an inner tube with nine cases of equipment tied to it on this side of the river, just before it floated south into Saddam-controlled Iraq. These people had gone into the luggage and found photocopies of two passports—which the governor now produces. He asks if I recognize the passport pictures. I look at them and smile. I say that one of them is my colleague and the other is me.

With that, the governor and his entourage breathe a huge sigh of relief and burst out laughing. They tell me they had assumed that the owner of the equipment had drowned. I am led down the corridor to a room where all the equipment is spread out on the floor—amazingly, all of it is in good condition except one Apple laptop computer, for which I have a replacement.

3/27/03

After two days of travel, I arrive with Pete in Sulaimaniya in northeastern Iraq, near Iran. We stayed last night in Arbil with the other CNN crews. It appears the war will not come to the north as expected, as the Turks have been reined in for the time

A Kurdish man stands in the marketplace in the town of Kifri, on the northern front line dividing Kurdish and pro-Saddam forces in Iraq.

being and the coalition strategy seems to be to take the south and then Baghdad. They're counting on the north to simply fold after victory in the south.

Tomorrow I'll go to Kifri, a town on the Iranian border one and one half hours from Baghdad.

Despite my earlier critical comments about the embedding process, I have been stunned by some of the pictures and footage that the embedded journalists and photojournalists have been getting. Nothing like it since Vietnam. There's a whole generation of Vietnam-trained soldiers now running the show, smart enough to know that their job is military and to let a free press inform the public.

03/28/03

Sulaimaniya is full of journalists, many of whom have been here for the last two months. I am happy to leave and head for a more remote locale. We drive down a road to Kifri, a town on the northern front line. I have a Bgan—a new hi-tech satellite modem—pointing out of my front car window. It will allow me to transmit data and images as we drive, since I have an antenna on the roof for a Thuraya satellite phone.

Ahead of me, the mountains loom on the horizon. The houses in the villages we pass are stone and cinderblock; the fields are green and lush; we see women in black robes with their heads shrouded and tattoos on their foreheads. Shepherds stand in the fields tending flocks of future shish-kebab.

One senses that there is a war, but so far there is no concrete sign of it anywhere I have been. And yet expectations that the fighting would be over fast seem to be fading. Twelve years of an American-led embargo against Iraq and a sense of defiance in response to the invasion of their country has led to more resistance than most people imagined.

Still, there is plenty of evidence that the Kurds are desperately ready for change. Earlier this afternoon, while we were setting up a videophone to connect to Atlanta, a man approached to show us several photocopied photographs and some text. He wanted us to know the terror that Ansar Al Islam, a fundamentalist ancillary group of Al Qaeda, had brought to this corner of the country. We also heard last night that six suicide bombers tried to enter Kurdistan from the extremist area near Halabjah, near Iran; three were shot and the other three arrested. And American paratroopers landed last night outside of Arbil and took over the airstrip.

We drive over a mountain and see below us a majestic vista of a shimmering lake. The sun is shining through the springlike, soft clouds. I just want to take some beautiful pictures. I would come back here again—in peacetime—to make images for myself of the power and natural grace that surrounds us.

We stop beside the road about thirty kilometers outside Kifri. The Mahmud Ahmed Abdullah family, seventy-four strong, are living in a field by the road in tents made from sticks and flour sacks. The family has a common trait: blue-green eyes. The old women have black tattoos on their faces, the younger women and girls wear black scarves over their heads, and the men have full, carefully trimmed moustaches and well-groomed eyebrows. The Mahmud Ahmed Abdullahs left Kifri because they were afraid of missile attacks (the front line is two kilometers away). They think the war will last twenty more days and they say the Iraqis are fighting because Saddam hangs insubordinate officers and the soldiers are afraid.

With the war raging around them, Kurdish men play dominoes in a cafe in the northern front-line town of Kifri.

The family is in favor of a free Kurdistan after Saddam. The men explain to me that they welcome the Americans as liberators but not the Turks. Despite their plight as refugees, we are immediately invited for tea. The dignity of these people is apparent; one of the elders of the clan had worked for an American company and wants to know if he can work for us.

I spend the late afternoon photographing in Kalar, a town thirty kilometers from the front line and about one and a half hours from Baghdad. There is an acute state of alarm throughout Kalar, and many Kurds are leaving the city for fear that Saddam will unleash chemical weapons on them. And yet their anxiety about being so close to the front line is mingled with a sense of anticipation and enthusiasm that the war will ultimately benefit this country and its people, despite the unknowns ahead.

We put up for the night with a Kurdish family, three generations of English teachers: father and mother, their two sons, and their granddaughter. They watch Fox TV and enjoy speaking English with each other. And they have an American perspective on their country. The grandfather explains, "For thirty-five years I have not been living comfortably. I have no car, no good life. Here you work your whole life just to survive. We are a rich country with more than twenty thousand oil wells but we don't get to enjoy any of these riches."

It is surreal to be watching Fox TV, drinking mint tea, and enjoying the warmth and hospitality of this Kurdish family so close to the fighting just south of us. Everybody crowds around us to eat the dinner laid out on a tablecloth on the sitting room carpet.

A Kurdish child stands in the Kifri marketplace during the war.

3/29/03

I wake up this morning to hear that in the south the American side will need a four- to six-day pause to resupply. My guess is that we will also use the hiatus to mount more of a presence here in the north. I photograph in the marketplaces of Kifri, the northern front border town. The people here scrutinize me in a different way than they did in other parts of Kurdistan, where everybody is always open and warm with Westerners. Here, we are just north of territory where the Al Qaeda group Ansar Al Islam has a base near Halabjah, where Hussein used chemical weapons against the Kurds in 1988. I don't know if the looks I get are due to my foreign appearance or whether I symbolize the presence of the Americans—a thousand paratroopers arrived nearby two days ago. Perhaps there is more tension here on the Iranian border, with the war looming.

Yesterday I attended a funeral for a man who had died of natural causes. The small, beautiful cemetery stirred memories of a number of funerals I have photographed around the world. My own sense of mortality is setting in at age forty-seven, and the cemetery and the grieving took on a strong meaning for me. I was reminded that I must live every day fully and appreciate my family and friends every second along the way.

03/30/03

It's early morning in Kalar, in the small house Pete and I have rented to cover the eastern side of the northern front. Our team is coming together: Salar, a recent college grad, bright and handsome, our translator and now chief live shot engineer; our driver, Sherwen, the oldest of the group; our peshmerga guards—Dilshad and Hunar, two brothers who could both be fashion models in New York or Paris; and our housekeeper, Ahmad, who everyone thinks talks too much. Seated together on the floor around a tablecloth, we finish breakfast.

The light is beautiful this morning. It is Sunday and spring is here; the weather has changed overnight. Driving down the roads reminds me of the landscape of the Karoo, a vast, flat, open prairie in South Africa, but with the trappings of the Mideast. Yesterday we were in Kifri. Coalition forces bombed the front lines there, and while we were on the roof of a peshmerga bunker two mortar shells fell a couple of hundred meters from our position. I spent the afternoon in the marketplace photographing people in the beautiful light. There are so many strong, proud faces in this town of little to do except smuggling.

Late last night we set up a live TV shoot. We were all jacked up and ready to go: I had Wolf Blitzer talking into my earphone; I had begun my delivery and was in mid-anecdote when the transmission line went dead and I went off the air. We'll try again in the morning.

Now, in a spare moment, I'm reading e-mails from friends and will call Charlie later.

I spend another afternoon in Kifri photographing more people in the market. I ask them to tell me about their lives. There's a widow in black who lost her whole family in a Saddam Hussein mustard gas attack on the town of Anfal in 1988; a soldier who earns $30 a month and who bought his Kalashnikov on the black market for $100; a retired house builder who spends his days playing *tawli,* a kind of backgammon; and a man whose five children sell eggs—thirty for $1.50—that he smuggles over the mountains by donkey from Iran.

Kurdish men sell gasoline on the black market in the town of Kalar, near the northern front.

On our way home, we see a militia group marching in formation, and we stop to get the story. They are not Kurds but Iraqi Arabs recruited from the south near Basra, members of the Iraqi National Congress financed by the United States. A Canadian guy of Iraqi descent comes out to speak to us. In perfect English, he says that the Americans have completely screwed up so far in this war and have gotten bogged down largely because the Turks wouldn't let them launch a northern offensive. A bit farther down the road, in a remote village off the beaten track, we encounter a house full of American special forces who refuse to talk to us.

I now think this war could go on for some time. A depressing thought. Spring is here and with its death and destruction, its crushing military hardware, this war is the antithesis of the season.

04/01/03

In Kifri I visit the local headquarters of PUK, the Kurdish political party that is popular in this area. After tea and lunch with the commanders, I leave with a brief and an aviation map detailing where the front line is spread across the north. We are about an hour from Baghdad, as the crow flies.

Overnight, the weather has changed directly from winter to summer, bypassing spring. Pete has bought our guards new pants, shirts, belts, and shoes. Their faces glow with delight. They have been so attentive, have tried so hard. I am sure the shoes that the younger brother chose are too small, but he is so proud to have them that he refuses to admit it.

We spend the afternoon visiting a front-line position where about a dozen peshmerga soldiers live in a small mud-packed bunker just outside a village. The Iraqi army is poised on a hill about two hundred meters away. We go into the village, where some three hundred families used to live. Only a few remain, the others having fled to the mountains for fear of a chemical weapons attack. This village is regularly shelled by the Iraqis, and the other night, when the coalition forces dropped bombs on the Iraqi positions, people said that "metal rained from the sky."

An elderly Kurdish woman prepares for a visitor in a nearly deserted village on the northern front line near the town of Kifri.

I am very melancholy today. Don't know if it is the weather here, but my heart feels heavy for the first time in several weeks even though I remind myself that we are still alive, breathing, our limbs intact. I realize that, like so many others, I have been deluded by thinking that this war would be over quickly. Now I figure it could take weeks, maybe months, with many dangerous days ahead. I've been on the road for two months; they've gone by fast, and yet I feel like I've been away from home a long time.

Kurds in the marketplace in Kifri.

04/02/03

In the late morning, we head for Kifri again. On the way I say to Pete that even though it's been quiet the last few days we should be careful about getting sucked into a false sense of security. Minutes later we encounter carloads of people racing out of town: during the night and early morning, American forces had bombed the so-called castle where the Iraqi army has its front-line position. The castle, only two hundred meters from town, took a direct hit, so the Iraqis retaliated by lobbing mortars into Kifri, killing at least three and injuring many others.

We rush into town and are directed to the home of a young schoolteacher who had been killed. We come upon a very dramatic scene. Following Muslim tradition, the men are behind a curtain in the backyard washing the body and preparing it to be wrapped in a white sheet for immediate burial. On the other side of the yard, three generations of Kurdish women are wailing in grief, pounding their chests, beating or scratching their faces, and angrily screaming "Saddam Hussein!" as they look skyward.

The body is taken into the house and the men kneel beside it. A wooden coffin is delivered, and after the corpse is laid inside, the family members throw themselves on the casket. Then, as the grieving women wail, it is put into a small truck and driven in a motorcade to the cemetery through what is now a ghost town.

I am accepted by the mourners into this most intimate of moments—why, I can only surmise. There are, perhaps, several reasons. The Kurdish people have

A young Kurdish soldier sits at a bunker that had just been taken over from Iraqi soldiers south of Kifri.

historically been disenfranchised, and their collective wish that their plight be recognized and addressed is likely one reason I've been allowed to witness and record their grief. I feel their need to shout their despair and to share this moment of mourning with those who understand. Perhaps, too, they recognize the camera as a way to memorialize the life of the person who has just passed. Finally, there is a sense of kinship we all feel because we are all exposed to the same risk of random death. I feel privileged to have such access to this moment. I can only hope that my pictures will do their small bit to arouse people everywhere to recognize and affirm life and to find an alternative to war.

Lofty ideals, perhaps, in the face of one family's tragedy. At times like these, I feel torn by conflicting emotions: I am moved by the unbelievable, almost theatrical beauty of what I am witnessing, but chilled by the thought that the slain teacher could have been me or a member of my family. I have a heightened awareness of the value of our ephemeral lives. One moment we share banalities; the next moment we are gone. I get to bed at about 4 A.M., still running on adrenaline after a physically and emotionally draining day.

04/04/03

After working in Kifri for days, Pete, Salar, Dilshad, and I drive through the marketplace. The Iraqis have finally retreated from their front-line position just outside of the town. They'd been lobbing shells into Kifri for the last seventy-two hours.

As we drive through town, people peer into the windows of our car, wave, and smile. They act as if we have liberated their city, or maybe they are simply recognizing us as being somehow associated with the Americans bombing the Iraqi front lines.

We stop for a cup of tea, and a man with a huge, touching smile suddenly walks over and kisses me on the cheek. He makes hand motions to represent an exploding bomb and points at me. Then I realize what he's trying to say. Everyone in town who got to know me while I was photographing in the marketplace knew that a cameraman had been killed the day before. They had assumed that I was that cameraman and are happy to see me alive.

Three more men come over and each give me sacks of fruit and vegetables and a kiss. The tea shop owner won't allow us to pay our bill, and I am as touched by their gestures as I am saddened by the death of the BBC cameraman. We find out later, when we visit the castle that the Iraqis had held, that he had driven off the road into the middle of a minefield.

We spend the rest of the day exploring the castle and an old police station, both overrun now with Kurdish peshmergas. We watch these fighters gleefully burn an Iraqi flag and tear a poster of Saddam Hussein to shreds. The peshmergas find logbooks with the names and birthplaces of the Iraqi troops who had occupied these positions. They also find craters from the American bombing.

The war is definitely gaining momentum. We hear that Americans are about to enter Baghdad and that our troops will finally be allowed to travel through Turkey into northern Iraq. Only a few days ago this war seemed interminable, but now I have a feeling that the coming days will go quickly and will bring rapid changes.

04/06/03

Yesterday morning I wanted to get some news, so I asked the man who has been bringing us food if I could visit his family to watch TV. When we got to his house, his nine-year-old sister Avin, who knew I had a son her age, wondered if I had spoken to him. She left for a moment, then returned with a red rose, which she gave to me. It aroused my appreciation for the beauty of a growing thing, the splendor of our natural world, in sharp contrast to the destruction and pain that I have been witnessing in this war.

In a nearly deserted Kurdish village on the northern front line, a Kurdish family makes tea for a visitor.

Last night we had a visit from another CNN crew, a good group of very driven itinerant professionals, including Brent Sadler. I was up on the roof of the house where we had

In the Kurdish town of Kifri, a relative grieves over the death of a twenty-six-year-old schoolteacher killed by Iraqi mortar shelling.

done a live shot, trying to feed some footage through a camera and a videophone. The stars were shining and the moon was overhead. Salar, our translator, was there. He's a young Kurdish mathematician, very self-contained, dignified, strong, full of initiative. We were having a beer when this smart young man took me by surprise. "David," he said, "I am twenty-five years old and I don't know what it will mean to live with freedom. I have no idea. I have never been anywhere outside of four towns in northern Iraq, and that is it."

I suddenly realized that all the talk about freedom, oppression, and democracy has not adequately addressed the fact that for thirty-five years this society has known nothing but one regime. I'm not so sure it has been fully appreciated that a change of government will bring its own challenges. And nobody really talks about what "freedom" means.

We visit a group of elderly Kurdish fighters in Kifri. Sitting with them, it suddenly becomes clear that this war is going to be over soon. It's a question of days: the Americans have entered Baghdad.

I ask one of the old men what he thinks about the war. He answers, "This military strategy has been so good. They haven't taken out electrical power or bridges. They've tried not to hit civilian areas." Whether this is true, I don't know. But I am overwhelmed to think that just possibly, in the midst of this horrible, destructive, divisive conflict, human lives have been considered.

Baghdad will fall any day now. My mind is on my next challenge: getting there, and staying safe while photographing the changes to the country and its capital. I also look forward to seeing my son, Charlie, soon. It has been a long week. The tragic death of the BBC cameraman really shook me up. The following day, the field where he died looked so peaceful. The townspeople had already put their past behind them, looking forward with excitement to peace and a new way of life. But I remain saddened by the loss of his life. I think about his family, about many others in this war whose lives have been changed from one day to the next, about the family histories and communities changed forever by the randomness of war.

I walk into Ibrahim's house, into the room where Pete, Salar, and I sleep along with Dilshad and Hunar, our Kurdish peshmerga guards.

It is after 1:00 in the morning. Pete and Salar are asleep. Dilshad and Hunar are sprawled out on the floor in front of the TV set with its new satellite dish we acquired yesterday to get some news, watching a European X-rated channel.

A relative pounds her chest, mourning the loss of a schoolteacher killed by Iraqi mortar shelling.

04/07/03

I'm a bit hungover from last night's wine and beer. I swallow three Nescafés and decide to go over to the local soccer field to exercise for an hour.

I am doing sit-ups when I hear a cow mooing. I moo back, then I imitate a sheep, a dog, a rooster, a cat; soon I'm surrounded by an entourage of twenty or so kids, and they mimic the sounds. It's more fun than I've had in a long time.

Later today I am downloading photographs from my computer when BBC's John Simpson reports on TV that a substantial convoy—including himself and a large contingent of peshmergas—had taken control of two Iraqi tanks moving along the front lines. The convoy was then spotted by an American airplane that dropped two bombs and killed eighteen people, among them a translator for the BBC and American special forces soldiers. Forty people were wounded, one of them the brother of the Kurdish leader Barsani.

Pete tells me the story of a British helicopter American ground troops mistook for an enemy helicopter and attacked with surface-to-air missiles that missed their target. The Brit landed, then strode over to the soldiers, with his white scarf blowing in the wind, and asked cooly if they had ever seen an Iraqi helicopter, and then he got back into his aircraft and flew off.

This morning I go to the market and ask a tailor to make some shirts for me and a little Kurdish costume for Charlie. I choose a beautiful material and find a boy his size for the fitting.

04/08/03

Back in Kifri today. Coalition forces report that they have found "Chemical Ali" dead in Basra. Chemical Ali was responsible for a mustard gas attack on Kurds in '88, when some five thousand people were killed in his attempt to "ethnically cleanse" the Kurds. Thousands taken from their homes never reappeared.

We do a standup interview in the streets with a man who has just returned from Baghdad, smuggling out a truck of rice. Like so many people, he's been smuggling for the last ten years, bringing in kerosene and petrol at great risk. Several of his relatives and friends were killed by the Iraqi military as they tried to make their way back north toward Kurdish territory. He tells me that his trip last night was the easiest in the last ten years because there is no longer an Iraqi military at checkpoints.

A Kurdish man stands in the Kifri marketplace.

In a tea shop, I interview the patrons about their reactions to Chemical Ali's death. "We are feasting here today at this news," one man says. After a moment he adds, "We are so excited that our freedom is coming now soon—that we can live in a democratic Iraq."

American troops are in Baghdad. Iraq's information minister announces on TV that Iraq is defending the airport and the city. Seconds later, a Pentagon briefing and CNN show pictures of tanks taking over the presidential palace, but news travels slowly in these regions. We stop at a small roadside stand to find that no one knows that the Americans are in Baghdad. One man suggests that the special forces bring in big TV screens and set them up in town squares throughout the country so the people know what is happening.

04/10/03

I spent yesterday once again trying to manage a computer crisis. I was on the terrace at 4:30 A.M., transmitting footage, when it started to rain. There was a power outage, then a surge, and the computer screen went black. I didn't sleep, knowing that it would be impossible to transmit my photographs.

All morning I've been drying the damn thing with a hair dryer. It still won't start, although the hard drive seems intact. I finally reached another CNN producer near here who was able to locate a spare laptop with another crew, and I spent another several hours on the phone with Atlanta getting it configured. Now it's about 4:30 P.M., Baghdad is falling, our TV shows American tanks in front of the Palestine Hotel in the center of the capital. I get a call from Earl Casey and Eason Jordan, at CNN, who thank me for my work but say that given what's happening in Baghdad they are pulling back crews, including mine. I tell them that in the next twenty-four hours I hope to make it to Baghdad if at all possible. There are lots of ifs: if the people here in the north know what is happening in the south, if we can get through the front lines, if we can avoid friendly fire as we head south. Eason gives me the green light, and we agree to speak again on Sunday to determine my next move. We run out the door to Kifri to see if we can find a way to get to Baghdad.

As the Iraqi army shells the Kurdish town of Kifri on the northern front line, a family flees the town with all of their belongings.

04/11/03

We made it a little way past Kifri yesterday, but had to go back. The peshmergas had taken a lot of territory, but the path south was still not open. Lots of excitement in the air, the anticipation of triumphant days to come, but so far no clear news about the situation at the front line. When we got back to the house, CNN was showing the scene outside the Palestine Hotel. Abrams tanks were arriving and taking charge in the middle of the city. Then we saw the dramatic footage that will become the iconographic image of the fall of Saddam: people toppling his statue, dragging the head through the streets of Baghdad.

The mood in our house is charged tonight. Everyone's keyed up: our guards, driver, and translator, all Kurds, are excited and anxious that we're heading for Baghdad. Of them, only the driver Sherwen has been in the capital, where he worked as a taxi driver. There's also a sense of jubilation over the fact that the man who has

A Kurdish fighter stares ahead after days of battle with the Iraqi army near Kifri.

ruled all their years in this country has just been deposed. At the same time, there's a feeling of melancholy. Everyone knows that soon we will part company and go our different ways.

Ibrahim cooks a big feast and we quietly sit together. After dinner, Hunar and Dilshad put on Kurdish TV, which shows people dancing in the streets, and they also start to dance, and Sherwen joins us. We all dance together, as Kurdish men do, with our hands in the air, sometimes linking little fingers.

By nightfall, the celebration in the neighborhood hits a high pitch with banging of tin drums, music, singing, and dancing. In the darkness, several hundred meters away, a party of Kurds dance together in the street, and drivers honk their horns as they go by. This is a society that generally segregates men and women, but tonight all come together to hold hands and share the language and joy of dance.

The women, usually in the background, have a clear sense of their powers of seduction when dancing. Pete, Salar, and I go over to photograph and are invited to join in. I find myself linking little fingers with a beautiful Kurdish woman on one side and a handsome Kurdish man on the other. This moment of joy no doubt is being shared by Kurds all across northern Iraq tonight as they celebrate their future.

We get a call at noon that Brent Sadler's crew has already headed south. I immediately go into high gear. We install the special racks we've had made for the roof of the car, to which we attach our satellite dishes so that we can transmit live as we drive south. We finish packing, share a last cup of tea, tie the luggage to the roof of the car, and cover it with white canvas on which we've painted "TV" in large letters. We shove off in a convoy of two vehicles for the south. Salar is with Pete and me in one car; in the other are Sherwen, the driver, and Hunar and Dilshad, our peshmerga guards.

We reach the town of Jabarah, which only that morning had been liberated. People rush out into the streets to cheer our arrival—the scene reminds me of Bucharest, Romania, when Ceaucescu was deposed. Down the road we meet a small contingent of American special forces and peshmergas who are moving forward very carefully. We follow them for ten kilometers until they stop in a village and invite us to visit the house of an important Arab in the village.

The visit to this gentleman is a scouting mission for the Kurds, who want to know if anyone in this predominantly Arab community has a car they can take over for the Kurdish Authority. The Kurds seem to be starting to take over Arab districts.

Refugees flee the Kurdish town of Kifri following an Iraqi army shelling attack on the city.

We are told not to go any farther south because on the outskirts of the village there are Iranian mujahideen who haven't yet retreated. So we backtrack a few kilometers and then make for a parallel, more westerly road that goes to Baghdad. We have about two hours of light left and want to push all the way. I sit on the roof of our Pajero hanging onto the luggage rack as we race south, taking in the truly beautiful countryside that spreads out in all directions.

As we approach the town of Jalula—which until this morning had been firmly in the control of the Iraqi army—we see dozens of armored vehicles and tanks that the Iraqis had simply parked on the side of the road. We also see many soldiers, and it starts to become difficult to distinguish the Iraqis who have surrendered from the Kurdish peshmerga who have taken over. Outside of this town of some 500,000 people, we see men looting refrigerators and taking every other conceivable booty from the local Iraqi army barracks. People jam the streets.

At dusk we head south again but run into another group of men, who warn that three hundred Iranian mujahideen are up the road and advise us to wait until tomorrow morning to continue on, so we return to Jalula. Sherwen pulls up in front of a villa and he, Pete, and I walk to the front door. An Arab gentleman greets us, and we ask if we can sleep in his house for the night. He doesn't hesitate to invite us in and introduces us to three of his children, his wife, and his parents.

We are ushered into a guest room, and then food is prepared and laid out on a tablecloth on the floor. A strong, very tall Iraqi sits near me. Later, I find out that he is our host's son-in-law, Hillal. I ask him how he feels about Saddam and the current situation. With sadness in his eyes, he says he doesn't want to speak of it. Still, he is gracious to us: the family then proceeds to serve us a veritable feast, and then accommodates us with beds and blankets.

The next morning, Hillal is in the foyer praying. He lays out another spread of food, and we sit down together to eat. I ask if he is a sportsman, and he smilingly admits that he had been the goalkeeper of the Iraqi national soccer team. Does he coach children? No, he says, he's been involved with the army, quietly acknowledging that he had been a colonel in a Republican Guard unit in Baghdad. He and his family arrived from the capital yesterday.

We talk for the next hour. He wonders if there could have been another way to disarm and remove Saddam Hussein without bombing and hurting so many people. I wonder as well, and we reflect on the heroic leadership that might have achieved this end less violently.

My crew and I must leave for Baghdad, and we are about ten kilometers south of Jalula when group of peshmergas stop us from going farther. They say that Iranian mujahideen are firing from the fields. We pull over and try to sort out what's really going on. Suddenly a Kurdish army jeep screeches to a stop with a fighter who has taken three bullets in the gut and one in the chest, just missing his heart. Pete, who has extensive medical training, grabs his first aid kit, and we help the man to the ground. Pete cuts through his bloodied shirt and seals the entry and exit wounds with plastic bandages. We put the man into the back of a truck, and he's rushed off to the hospital.

We hit the road again. The farther south we go, the more intense the scene around us becomes. We continuously meet up with Kurdish peshmergas who tell us to turn back because they have been shot at. Then we meet Iraqi Arabs who insist that the peshmergas are looting Arab towns. But we keep going. The beautiful countryside is littered with abandoned tanks. We pull into the town of Al Khalis, with me still on the roof of the car. In the other towns we'd driven through, we had quickly gotten the sense that the tide had turned: the murals of Saddam Hussein had been defaced, and people had cheered us when we arrived. But here the murals of Saddam remain—and nobody's cheering. At an intersection men in civilian clothes with Iraqi flags around their shoulders are checking all the vehicles. Several spot me, no one smiles, and they look like hawks sighting prey. A man about twenty meters away points his AK-47 in my

Kurdish women grieve the death of a relative in a cemetery outside of Kifri.

direction and, shouting something unintelligible, starts running toward our car. If there ever was a life-or-death situation, this is it.

Kurdish men sit in the marketplace.

I dive into the car, pushing aside the video camera so as not to damage it, and scream to Pete to step on the gas. Salar, in the passenger seat, also dives to the floor. Gunfire blasts in our direction as Pete screeches through the intersection. The car is weaving and dodging—it's like a scene from a bad movie, with bullets whizzing by. Flattened against the floor, I keep thinking that any minute now I'm going to feel a bullet come through the door and go through me.

Pete races the car forward about three hundred meters to another checkpoint with a traffic light and men stopping cars. With the gunmen chasing us, Pete makes a sharp right turn and careens down a street directly toward an army barracks, where Saddam's image looms on a huge poster. Seems to me that we're heading straight for a hornet's nest. How can we get out of this? I have the desperate notion that our only option is to ask a family somewhere for refuge. I yell to Pete, "What are you thinking?" Pete yells back, "I think we are in the shit, that's what I'm thinking!"

Somehow, we get back on the main road, having bypassed the traffic light, and find ourselves speeding through town, heading south into the countryside. A car is coming up fast behind us, and someone yells that the car carrying Sherwen, our driver, and Hunar and Dilshad had escaped the dangers of Al Khalis by turning off onto a side road and taking a detour north.

There's no turning back now. But as we move south, we realize that the rest of the route to Baghdad is probably not liberated and that we will probably run into more of the same. We reach another small town and another roundabout where the traffic is stopped. In an instant, we're encircled by a dozen armed Iraqi men in kaffiyehs. This time, though, I catch someone's eye and he smiles. I motion to him to get in the car with us; he does, and to our relief, all the other armed men defer to our unknown passenger's authority and escort us out of town.

I am holding Pete's navigator, which indicates that we're only forty minutes from Baghdad. There don't appear to be any more towns between us and the capital. I call the international desk at CNN in Atlanta and describe our situation. They're worried: no other news crews have been south on this road. They have just heard about another crew that was robbed and beaten near Chamchamal—among them Mitch the New Zealander, my fellow traveler across the river into Iraq.

We stay in phone contact with Atlanta as we rush south. Masses of vehicles are heading in both directions, crammed with family members and all their belongings. The closer we get to the capital, the more cars clog the roads. We are the first Westerners to appear on this route since the war began, and people stare at us with suspicion, fear, and anger. Smoke from oil fires blackens the horizon; there is an intense afternoon light, an ominous, almost monochromatic charcoal blue sky.

The navigator reads nine minutes to Baghdad. With the city spread out in front of us, the roads congested and chaotic, I fear that we are driving into another ambush. Then, in a field to my left, I see an enormous arsenal of military equipment that belongs to the marines. We've hit the perimeter! We pull over when we see a group of our troops and report where we've come from. They can't believe we've forged our way along that treacherous route. After a few moments to stretch and collect ourselves, we're back on the congested road, heading south, this time following a marine convoy into Baghdad. From my rooftop perch, I look out on scenes of destruction, streams of refugees, oil well fires.

The marine convoy pulls over, but we drive on toward the city center. We find a man who speaks English and ask him to take us to the Palestine Hotel. He hops into his car, and we follow him through burning Baghdad neighborhoods. Massive murals of Saddam Hussein are plastered everywhere, and Baghdadis push shopping carts stuffed with loot through the streets to the sound of sporadic machine-gun fire in the distance.

A Kurdish women stands in the doorway of her home following the shelling of her town, Kifri.

Ten minutes later, we pull up in front of the Palestine Hotel, where only two days earlier the statue of Hussein had come crashing down.

In the lobby, I meet Patrick Robert, a French photographer I've known for years. He calls me Peter, my twin's name.

I move on through the lobby. I see Peter wearing a flak jacket, his face tanned, his long blond hair bleached lighter from days in the sun. There's nothing new in this encounter: we've been meeting in war zones for years, and we hug, feeling the bond and intimacy unique to twins.

I check in, Peter goes up with me to my room, and I help him transmit his photographs to the *Denver Post*. I send my own photographs to CNN, then do a live standup on the hotel roof. Back in my room, I discover Salar fast asleep, stretched out naked on one of the beds. Pete sprawls on a mattress on the floor; I crawl under the sheets and am out for the count in Baghdad.

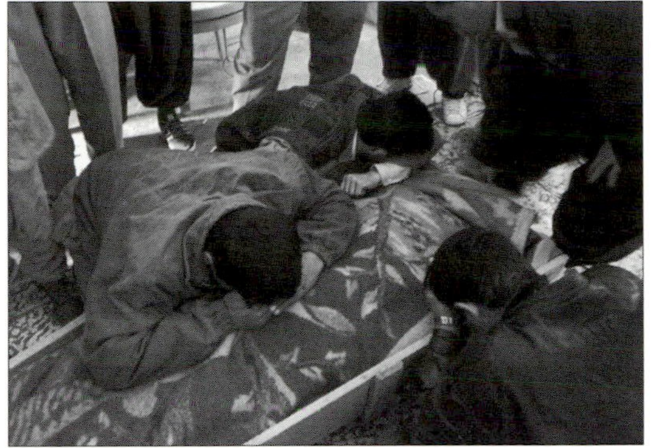

The family of a schoolteacher throw themselves on his body.

04/13/03

We hit the streets to photograph. I had been here in 1991, before and after the first Gulf War, and again in 1996. I can immediately tell that the mood has changed. After a twelve-year embargo and another war, the Arabs seem to be drained, no longer exhibiting the generosity and curiosity toward foreigners that I remember. Instead, there is a look of real concern over where to get water or food in a city without electricity, a government, or a police force. And for now, the only manifestation of freedom seems to be the right to loot. I see people gleefully racing out of former government buildings toting cabinets, chairs, light fixtures—you name it. People come up to me constantly with the same message: "Tell George Bush we are waiting: waiting for a new government, for food to eat, and a return to order." What Baghdadis seem to fear now is having no sense of what comes next. A small girl walks by me with two AK-47 ammunition clips. Men exchange bundles of Iraqi dinars for dollars. At the marketplace, there are only a few potatoes, tomatoes, and apples. People are opening fire hydrants to bathe, and they're taking water back home in buckets.

04/14/03

Up at 6 A.M. I go to the hotel across the street where my brother is staying. I hadn't seen him in three months, and I know he had a tough time in the south. As a

Kurdish soldiers take over a bunker that had only hours before been occupied by the Iraqi army just south of Kifri.

photojournalist—unattached to an American military unit—he found it hard to find places to sleep or food to eat, and the work was dangerous, but he, too, had made the decision not to be embedded. As I knock on the door to his room, Eric Feferburg, a wonderful French photographer, shows up. Peter lets us into his gear-filled room, his cozy bunker in the middle of a chaotic war zone.

The three of us speak in French, sharing our war stories. I love to hear my brother speak with such passion and thirst for life, describing his adventures in vivid detail.

My brother asks me if I want to work with him today, and I am torn, because we haven't worked together in a long time. Somehow, I feel that our Karma will be strongest if we continue to work separately, and my intuition is not to change that dynamic now.

Later this morning, I am in the old city doing interviews. Before coming to Baghdad, I imagined that I would see American tanks driving through this part of town, but I don't see American troops. I am wondering if the old city is not considered a strategic zone when suddenly American tanks come rolling along the pavement and barrel through the ancient quarter, a roaring convoy of monsters. I spin around and make one of my most memorable photographs of this war, showing Iraqis, in particular a young girl, cheering the arrival of the troops. It's serendipitous, but I believe that if I just keep working with concentration, purpose, and discipline I will be in the right place at the right time, ready to capture these memorable events.

Later in the day, with Pete and Salar, I go to one of Saddam's palaces along the Tigris—the one where he actually lived much of the time. U.S. marines patrol the perimeter of the kilometer-square compound, ostensibly keeping journalists out. Nonetheless, they let me in when I flash my CNN credential. Pete and Salar wait in the car. For the first time in weeks I am alone, walking in the bright sunlight through the stunning and immense landscape that was Saddam's backyard, enjoying solitude and peace in the midst of the chaos of Baghdad.

I pass by a tank with a single American soldier sitting on top. We start to talk. He's from Warsaw, Indiana, minutes away from where my mother lives. When I tell him I had played football for Fort Wayne Elmhurst, my high school in Indiana, we really connect. He says he's going home to visit his mom in Indiana as soon as he gets out of Baghdad.

I continue my walk to Saddam's "house"—a gargantuan palace with a huge arched entryway and a colossal gold chandelier. The front steps are thick with the stone dust that settled after the palace was bombed. I walk through it photographing remnants of opulent rooms with marble floors and walls of inlaid ivory, spaces the size of high school gymnasiums. Inside, I bump into a Romanian journalist and we swap deposed-dictator stories. She describes her tour of Ceaucescu's mansions after the fall of Bucharest in 1989, and I tell her about being in Ceaucescu's office with the militia who had taken over the Romanian presidential palace, all of us watching his execution on a TV screen. We walk together through the palace and find Saddam's bedroom, an auditorium-sized room with a marble floor. I stretch out on a luxurious divan. Then I relieve myself in Saddam's gold-plated toilet.

A Kurdish man smokes a cigarette in the marketplace of Kifri.

04/15/03

Today is my last day in Baghdad.

I've been on the road almost three months, and my body is only now starting to release the deep tensions that result from being constantly alert and from the relentless concentration it takes to do my work. I'm also unwinding from the strain of sharing a room with two other men for the last month, of being so far from loved ones, and from the pain of witnessing the devastation and disillusionment this war has brought to the lives of so many people.

Last night, in search of a computer cable, I went to Peter's hotel and called his room from downstairs. I asked him how things were going, and he told me that he had just experienced the saddest moment of his professional career. He had been at a hospital when a father came in with his beautiful eleven-year-old daughter suffering from pulmonary pneumonia. He had been unable to get her to the hospital until then because of the war, and the doctors tried to resuscitate her, to no avail; she died in front of them. I went to his room to hug him—and be hugged.

This morning, around 6:00, I go to the CNN workspace where Christiane Amanpour has just finished her live shots for the night. We talk for quite a while—the way we used to years ago.

Our conversation makes me realize how anxious I am about going home—back to the hustle and bustle of New York, back to puzzling over what to do next with my life as I head into my forty-eighth year. I'm anxious, too, about being a good father to Charlie and about continuing to exercise my professional skills in ways that keep me engaged. This is clearly too much to sort out today, but I can't stop thinking. Working in a war zone provides a photojournalist with a sense of daily purpose. Other people's lives, dreams, and tragedies become so important; they keep everything in perspective. They spur us to underscore in our work the value of life, love, and family. I suppose what I fear most is to return to the banality of a life that provides all the modern amenities without a strong sense of meaning or mission.

But enough reflection. I must embrace this moment with gratitude, gratitude to Eason Jordan and CNN for having supported my work in the field and given me such a tremendous opportunity to learn and to have a voice, gratitude to my family and friends who have been so concerned for me, to my mates who have been with me through thick and thin these last three months, to Pete and Salar, and to Jack Van Antwerp, who worked with me in Syria and Turkey. Gratitude for the opportunity to see my brother, Peter, so vibrant and fulfilled in his work, and gratitude for the opportunity to share life with so many wonderfully passionate, sensitive photojournalists and journalists, who have given so much of themselves and remain true to their convictions in spite of enormous risks, sometimes losing their lives.

Kurdish soldiers stand inside a bunker they have just won from the Iraqi army during intensive fighting outside the town of Kifri.

After writing these words on this, my last night in Iraq, I go to the hotel "restaurant" for a bite. The place has no electricity, and usually no food. Still, it has become a hangout for journalists and soldiers who come in to get off the street and spend time in somewhat more peaceful and familiar surroundings.

South of Baghdad, an American armored personnel carrier patrols a route being used by thousands of Iraqis walking from the south back toward the capital following the fall of Saddam Hussein.

Lit by a gasoline-powered generator, the restaurant is dim, the decor tattered and dreary. I talk to a young man who works for the *Denver Post*. Bone-weary, I struggle to concentrate; I think about leaving Baghdad for Kuwait early in the morning. Suddenly, I'm caught off guard by the sound of a piano. I know that it is not the Middle Eastern music I've been hearing for the last three months, and when I turn around I see a U.S. marine at the piano, a young Hispanic in a dirt-stained chocolate chip uniform, helmet, and flak jacket, his machine gun slung over his shoulder. He stares dreamily ahead, his body language slowly changing from that of a stiff-backed soldier to that of a man losing himself in his music. He starts to riff, first something light and tentative; then a little Motown; then the blues.

People start drifting in to see where the music is coming from. All at once there's a full house, with everyone listening silently, mesmerized by the rhythms, the spirit of the melodies. The notes speak of life, sadness, and affirmation, of the desire to keep moving on, as the young man taps out a soft, swaying, sometimes joyful ballad on a piano in a dark corner of a room in the heart of war-torn Iraq.

Within minutes, the piano is surrounded by soldiers, all with weapons slung over their shoulders: men with dusty faces, white, Hispanic, Asian, black—all young Americans in a faraway place now connected to home by the familiar beats of music their ears and hearts have known since childhood.

And then it is over. The piano player gets up to go. As he passes my table, I thank him for his beautiful music. He tells me he is from south-central Los Angeles and that he learned to play the piano in a church where his father is a Baptist minister. He seems surprised and a bit embarrassed by the impact his music has had on the crowd. He responds to my appreciation with a soft "Thank you, sir," puts on his helmet, and turns to go back out into the midnight streets of a restless city. Baghdad Blues.

RİKET-
MENT
ALIM S

چایخانەی
فەرەیدون
بەخیرهاتنتان دەکات

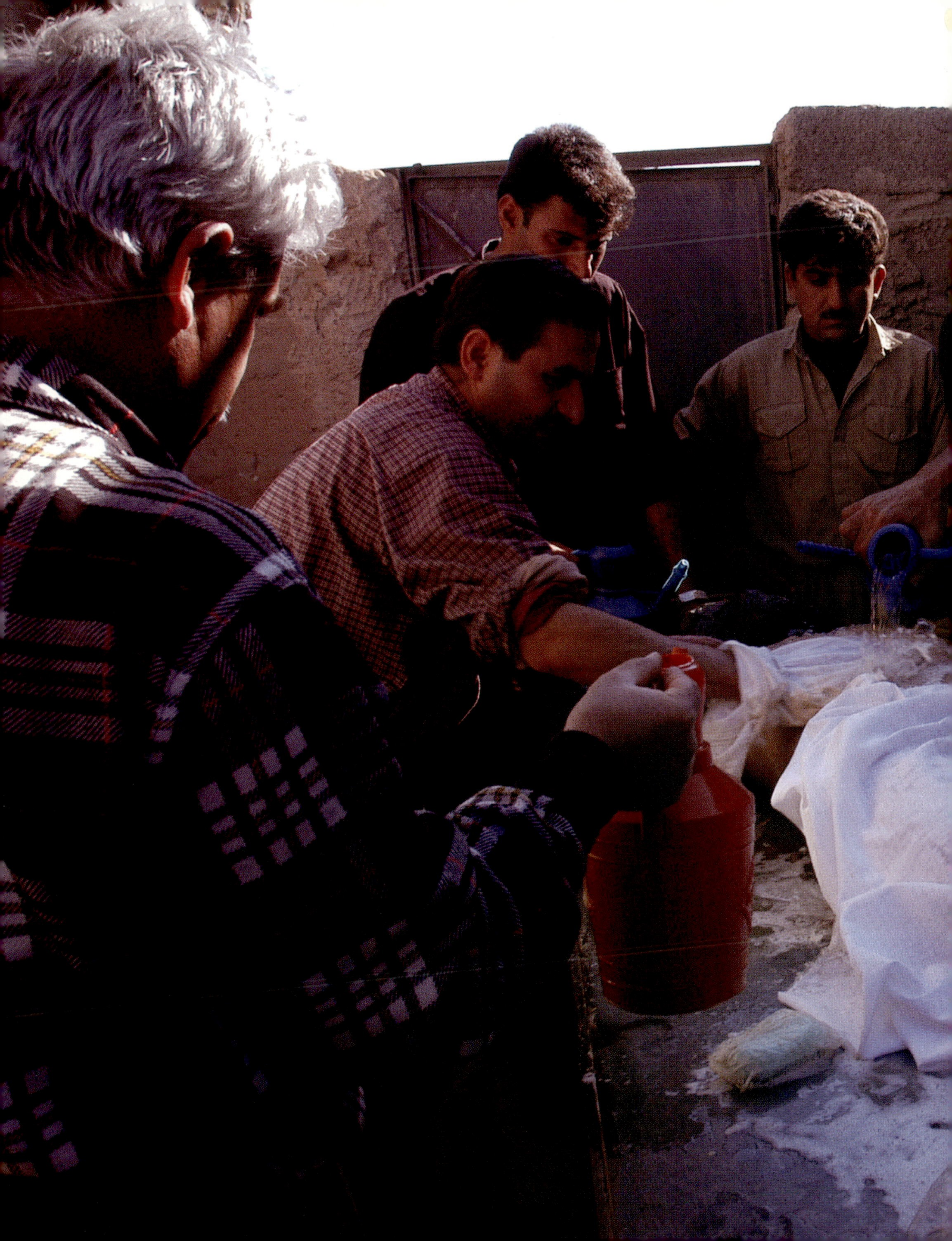

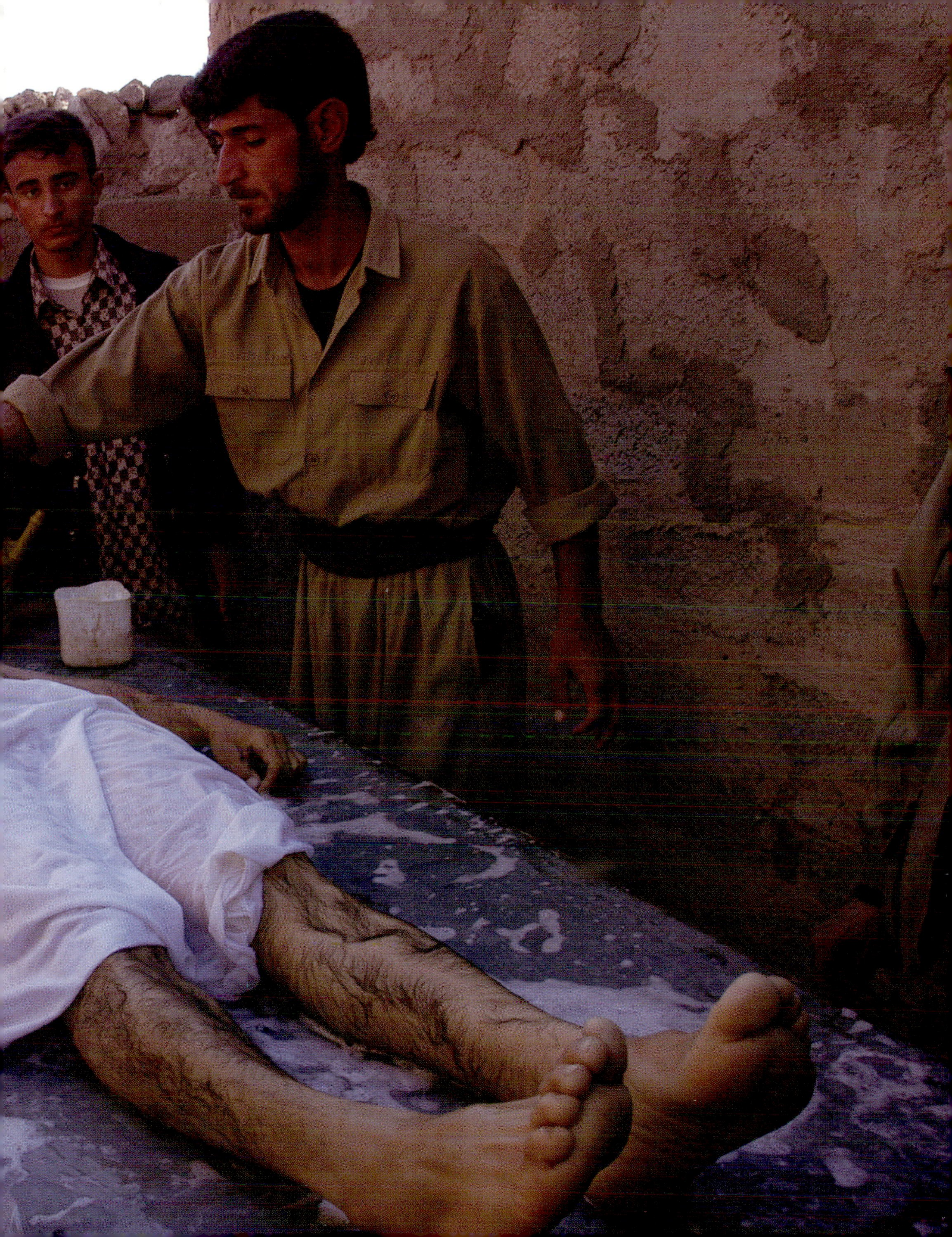

SSR 76
7.00-16
SEMIRIB

aksa

فندق البتول

41

ABOUT THE PHOTOGRAPHS

PAGE 1: Along the Turkish border with Iraq, a Kurdish woman and her child return to the village of Handek after working in the fields.

PAGES 2–3: American soldiers check vehicles moving south down a highway from Baghdad in southern Iraq following the fall of Saddam Hussein.

PAGES 4–5: A Kurdish family at home in the Turkish village of Handek along the border with Iraq.

PAGES 40–41: In a Kurdish town inside Turkey on the way to northern Iraq, Kurdish men sit in a café playing cards, smoking cigarettes, and drinking Turkish coffee.

PAGES 42–43: A pitcher stands on a table in a Kurdish shish-kebab restaurant in Turkey.

PAGES 44–45: Two Kurdish friends walk through an alleyway in the Turkish town of Czire near the border with northern Iraq.

PAGES 46–47: Kurdish men sit in a coffee shop in the Turkish town of Czire discussing the prospect of war.

PAGES 48–49: A Kurdish man stares into the camera in a restaurant in a town in Turkey on the way to northern Iraq.

PAGES 50–51: In the Turkish village of Handek, a Kurdish father kisses his child, who rests in a cradle inside the family's home.

PAGES 52–53: A Kurdish schoolgirl adjusts her scarf outside her family's home in Handek near the border with northern Iraq.

PAGES 54–55: Kurdish children play in the mud in the rain soaked Turkish village of Handek.

PAGES 56–57: Kurdish children play with a goat in Handek.

PAGES 58–59: A Kurdish girl stands outside her family's mud home in the mountains along Turkey's border with Iraq.

PAGES 60–61: A Turkish schoolteacher supervises Kurdish children playing soccer along the border with northern Iraq.

PAGES 62–63: A Kurdish woman fetches water from the village well in Handek.

PAGES 64–65: A Kurdish child stands in the mud in front of his family's tent in the mountain village of Handek near the Iraqi border.

PAGES 66–67: A Kurdish man and his wife sit near their wood-burning stove in Handek.

PAGES 68–69: A Kurdish boy walks along a path through the village of Handek.

PAGES 70–71: In a one-room schoolhouse that serves the entire village of Handek, Kurdish schoolchildren greet a visitor.

PAGES 72–73: Kurdish men and women dance during a wedding celebration outside of the Turkish town of Czire near the border with northern Iraq.

PAGES 74–75: A Kurdish woman at a wedding ceremony.

PAGES 76–77: Kurdish women dance in a wedding ceremony.

PAGES 78–79: A Kurdish man prays during a wedding.

PAGES 80–81: A Kurdish fighter patrols the streets of Kifri during the war.

PAGES 82–83: Kurds in the marketplace in Kifri.

PAGES 84–85: Breakfast in the home where I stayed with my crew in the Iraqi Kurdish town of Kalar near the northern front line.

PAGES 86–87: An elderly man in the marketplace in Kifri.

PAGES 88–89: Kurdish men play dominoes and drink coffee in the marketplace of Kifri.

PAGES 90–91: A Kurdish man serves a cup of tea to a visitor in Kifri.

PAGES 92–93: A Kurdish refugee child looks into the camera on the outskirts of Kifri, which her family had fled to avoid the chemical attack they anticipated from Saddam Hussein's forces.

PAGES 94–95: A Kurdish girl stands outside the tent that had become the home of her family after fleeing Kifri.

PAGES 96–97: Outside of Kifri, which had just been shelled by the Iraqi army, one of the thousands of Kurdish refugees who had fled the town sits in his wheelchair alongside the road leading from town.

PAGES 98–99: Following Muslim tradition, Kurdish men cleanse the body of the young teacher killed in an Iraqi shelling attack, preparing it for burial.

PAGES 100–101: Relatives of a twenty-six-year-old Kurdish schoolteacher killed by an Iraqi shelling attack grieve his death in the northern front-line town of Kifri.

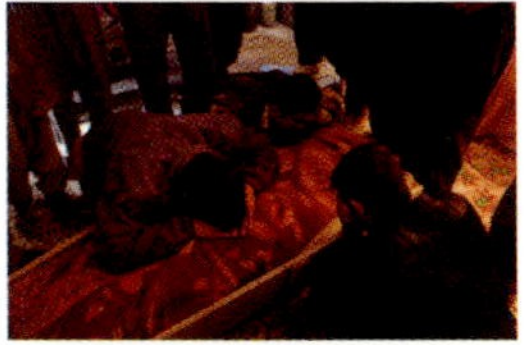

PAGES 102–103: A relative of a young teacher mourns his death.

PAGES 104–105: Relatives throw themselves on the teacher's body before burial.

PAGES 106–107: Kurdish fighters take aim at Iraqi army positions on the south side of the northern front-line town of Kifri.

PAGES 108–109: A Kurdish couple flees Kifri during Iraqi shelling with their children and all of their belongings.

PAGES 110–111: A young Kurdish fighter sits inside a bunker he and his fellow soldiers had captured from the Iraqis during intense fighting on the southern edge of Kifri.

PAGES 112–113: An elderly Kurdish man stands in thought during the war.

PAGES 114–115: After driving the Iraqi army from the southern edge of Kifri, Kurdish townspeople display the spoils of war that the soldiers left behind when they retreated.

PAGES 116–117: Kurdish families that had just fled the shelling of Kifri find refuge in a field several kilometers north of the town.

PAGES 118–119: Kurdish fighters stand outside their bunker on the southern edge of Kifri.

PAGES 120–121: As Saddam Hussein's regime was falling, Kurdish shepherd children ride a donkey along the highway leading to Baghdad from the north.

PAGES 122–123: Driven from Kifri by an Iraqi shelling attack, a Kurdish family takes refuge in a field north of the town.

PAGES 124–125: Seemingly oblivious to the war, a young Kurdish boy leads his flock of sheep along a highway near the northern front.

PAGES 126–127: A Kurdish fighter is pulled from a jeep after being shot along a highway by pro-Iraqi Iranian mujahideen; he was hit in the stomach and chest by four bullets.

PAGES 128–129: A Kurdish man along a highway heading toward Baghdad expresses his glee at Saddam Hussein's loss of power.

PAGES 130–131: Kurdish children cheer the fall of Hussein on the road heading south to Baghdad.

PAGES 132–133: Fires blaze on the horizon in Baghdad on the northern edge of town when the Iraqi government lost control of the city.

PAGES 134–135: An Iraqi woman walks with her belongings on her head as she returns to Baghdad from the south following the fall of Hussein.

PAGES 136–137: Children stand near a mural of Hussein following the arrival of American troops in Baghdad.

PAGES 138–139: Looking for water to drink, an Iraqi man stares into space in the old city of Baghdad.

PAGES 140–141: Iraqis cheer the arrival of a convoy of armored personnel carriers in the old city of Baghdad.

PAGES 142–143: Sheltered for days during the war in their apartment in Baghdad, an Iraqi family comes out into the sunlight on their terrace after American troops have entered the city.

PAGES 144–145: A mural of Saddam Hussein outside an art institute where artists painted portraits of the ex-president.

PAGES 146–147: A boy plays a broken upright piano in the schoolyard of an elementary school in Baghdad following the fall of Saddam Hussein.

PAGES 148–149: Walking for many kilometers, Iraqi women return to Baghdad from the south after American troops have taken over Baghdad.

PAGES 150–151: A young Iraqi girl walks through the rubble following the bombing of Baghdad.

PAGES 152–153: Iraqis beat and burn an effigy of Hussein in the old city of Baghdad.

PAGE 160: An American soldier, who spoke no Arabic, and an Iraqi, who spoke no English, share a moment on the southern edge of Baghdad following the fall of Hussein.

ACKNOWLEDGMENTS

At Vendome Press, special thanks to my dear friend and publisher Mark Magowan, and to Alex Gregory, Isabel Venero, Hope Koturo, and Sarah Davis.

There are so many people at CNN who provided me with the most professional support and friendship while in the field. They include:

Eason Jordan, Teya Ryan, David Bohrman, Aaron Brown, Amanda Townsend, Paula Kim, Earl Casey, Parisa Khosravi, Lynn Felton, Jim Sutherland, Richard Griffiths, Gavin Owen-Thomas, Arnie Christianson, Ann Hoevel, Michael Schulder, Cynthia Salinas, Tom Fenton, Lonzo Cook, Robert Padavick, Maria Dugandzic, Andrew Henstock, Paul Ferguson, Waffa Munayyer, Dan Young, Christiane Amanpour, Nic Roberston, Jim Clancy, Ingrid Formanek, Brent Sadler, Christian Streib, Maria Fleet, Ben Wedeman, Mary Rogers, Kim Norgaard, Ken Robinson, Kevin Sites, Bill Skinner, Talia Kayali Larry Register, Martin Savage, Tomas Etzler, Steve Cassidy, Carol Cassidy, David Clinch, Eli Flournoy, Lisa King, Douglas Wood, Will King, Deborah Kaufman, Aneesh Raman, and Ayman Mohyeldin.

Special thanks to my mates Pete Hornett, Jack Van Antwerp, Salar, Mitch, and Chas, who traveled with me at different times along the way during my three months in the Middle East. To all of the wonderful colleagues I spent three weeks in Turkey with, thank you for keeping my spirits up with your great company.

At Corbis, who represented my photographs from the war, I would like to thank my friends Steve Davis, Brian Storm, Rick Boeth, David Laidler, and Justin Burke.

Thank you to Dirck Halstead, and Marc Kermisch for the great work you do with the digitaljournalist.org, which showcased the work of so many respected photojournalists from the war.

Thanks to Lora Myers and Constance Herndon, who edited my words and kept my voice.

My gratitude to Laura Lindgren, who so beautifully designed this book and is a pleasure to work with.

To Per Gylfe, thank you for the wonderful artistry preparing my photographs for publication.

To all of my personal friends and family—I want to thank you from the bottom of my heart for being there and for worrying about me while I was away.

And to my son Charlie—you make every day a joy for me